Islamic Banking—
A $300 Billion Deception

Islamic Banking— A $300 Billion Deception

Observations and Arguments on Riba (interest or usury), Islamic Banking Practices, Venture Capital and Enlightenment.

Dr. Muhammad Saleem

To order additional copies of this book, contact:
Xlibris Corporation
1-888-795-4274
www.Xlibris.com
Orders@Xlibris.com
31187

Contents

INTRODUCTION

The Islamic banking phenomenon, started in earnest in the 1980s, and currently Islamic banks control at least $300 billion in assets. The underlying rationale is based on their interpretation that Quran forbids interest—whether it is 1% per annum or 20%. The actual word in the Quran for interest or usury is riba. Islamic banks, on the basis of their interpretation that riba is interest, have responded by introducing a number of products which they claim are Sharia compliant or based on the concept of profit and loss sharing.

This book will attempt to address two issues: first whether the verses in the Quran concerning riba referred to normal interest or to usury which can be defined as interest above the legal or socially acceptable rate. In evaluating and discussing this point I believe it is important to keep in mind the pre Islamic lending practices, in other words the context as well the special historical circumstances in which the Quran was revealed in the 7th century Arabia. Muslims should be prepared to debate this issue, not simply accept judgments, fatwas, and views of religious scholars and Mullahs, many of whom are blissfully unencumbered with any knowledge of Islamic history, economics and banking.

The second point raised in this book is, that even if, for the sake of argument, one accepts the interpretation of the boosters of Islamic banking that Islam forbids all interest, is what the Islamic banks are practicing, in the name of Islamic banking, Islamic? Are the Islamic banking products and modes of financing truly Sharia complaint in both letter and spirit? Currently much—as much as 80%—of Islamic banking is done on the basis of Murabaha. Murabaha is essentially a trading transaction and banks have adopted this mode of financing because Quran encourages trading but not riba (interest or usury), even though the banks are not trading organizations. The central idea of Islamic banking is supposed to be that banks should share in the risk of the business with their clients and in order to achieve this goal their lending/investing transactions should be done on a profit and loss sharing basis as partners with their clients, not as lenders. How much of their total business is being done on the Musharaka and Mudaraba—the two truly profit and loss sharing modes of Islamic financing? These two are also similar to the Western financing techniques of venture capital financing.

Implicit in the idea of forming Islamic banks is that in addition to the presumed ban on interest, Islamic banking is a superior banking system to the Western banking system. Have the Islamic banks been able to demonstrate that this self imposed segregated system has contributed to greater equality, justice and fairness in the Muslim communities?

Also explored is the contribution, if any, to economic development the Islamic banking institutions have made since their inception some 30 years ago, even though for many this was not a primary reason for establishing the banks; the primary reason being their promotion of Islamization in its early days, although one suspects the motive has changed for most players in recent years. In any event, the Islamic banks should be asked whether their "sharia compliant" way of meeting the needs of the Muslim community has made any differences to the lives of people or resulted in increasing the level of compassion and justice in the Muslim societies?.

Finally in the concluding section I offer a set of policy recommendations for the Islamic banks, challenging them to reform their lending and investing practices to 1) only focus on the type of lending that can be done without interest, suggesting that they get more actively involved in venture capital (essentially musharaka and mudaraba) leaving the interest based type of lending or engage in this transparently and honestly like conventional banks.

This book is based largely on author's personal experience with one of the largest Western banks and a leading Islamic bank. While I was at the Islamic bank, I was a member of the management, credit and loan committees. And of course I have also seen much of the documentation used by the Islamic banks. Additionally, a good deal of the information presented comes from my friends currently working in Islamic banks in the Middle East. So in a sense it is an insider's story, albeit from the point of one who having observed the Islamic banking scene has become extremely disillusioned and alarmed at the level of dishonesty and deception being practiced in the name of Islam.

I would like to confess here that as it relates to religious matters, I speak as a Muslim layman, so if I have misunderstood Islamic history, the message of the Quran, or The context and /or misinterpreted the verses concerning riba, I ask God's forgiveness. Finally, although I am critical of the Islamic banking practices, and skeptical of their efforts and intent, I write in the spirit of constructive criticism. And that is the reason I have gone to some length to offer some policy recommendations. Simply put, what the Islamic banking industry needs is enlightenment. That can only come from first shedding some light on their existing practices and then as a second step to start doing the right thing which is truly consistent with the teachings of the Quran and which will add additional value.

RIBA—USURY OR INTEREST

Proponents of Islamic banking say that Islam bans all interest. But an understanding of pre-Islamic and Islamic history and keeping in mind the context, would lead one to conclude that what the Quran bans is usury, not interest. Usury can be defined as interest above the legal or socially acceptable rate. Phrased differently usury is the exploitative, exorbitant interest rate.

Individuals and institutions borrow money for two reasons: Either an individual needs to borrow money to pay bills, purchase food, pay for rent, clothing etc (consumptional purposes) or to borrow for an investment on which he expects to earn a rate of return higher than the cost of funds—call it interest—charged by a financial institution or a money lender. In the latter category of possible investments the list is endless but these would include, buying stock of listed company, setting up of a factory, opening a grocery store, a leverage buy out or an equity transaction, purchase of a rental property or investment property, bonds, and derivative products of all shapes and sizes. So borrowing is for either consumption purposes or for investment purposes.

It is safe to assume that the Mecca and Medina economy of 7th century lacked banks, much less such sophisticated and complicated financial products and instruments as those mentioned above. Therefore it is further safe to assume that in the Arabia Peninsula of 7th century the motivation for borrowing was for consumption purposes or based on need—a poor person in distress needing to borrow money from a rich person, since there were no financial institutions existing at that time. This implied that the rich money lender was in a stronger position than the borrower, which led to many abuses on the part of the lenders. The lenders had the upper hand and the borrowers were at the mercy of such lenders. Such lenders in pre-Islamic period would charge exorbitant and exploitive interest. In many cases the borrowers saw their debt double or triple if they were not able to pay on time. This was called riba, or usury. Money lenders throughout Islamic history have charged interest ordinary interest and it was not until the Islamic banks opened their doors for business in the 1980s that the issue of riba even became a subject of serious discussion. Increasingly with the move toward Islamization in many Islamic countries, many scholars have equated riba with interest. It is a completely wrong interpretation but one that has become quite widespread in the last 30 years, even though many learned scholars—notably M.A.S. Abdel Haleem and Arthur J. Arberry—in translating the Quran from Arabic to English have translated riba to mean usury, not normal interest.

Islam is not the only religion that prohibits usury—exorbitant and/or exploitative interest. The history of usury is thousands years old. In India going back some 4000 years, lenders were advised not to exploit the poor and the Old Testament delivered the same message. All main religions of the world, including Hinduism, Buddhism, Judaism, Christianity and Islam have negative things to say about the practice. Usury has been repeatedly condemned, prohibited, scorned, and restricted, mainly on moral, ethical, religious grounds. Surprisingly, Adam Smith, despite widely known as the "father of the free market capitalism" came out strongly in support of controlling usury, essentially advocating the imposition of an interest rate ceiling.

Riba or usury—a pre-Islamic practice—indeed is sinful and evil, because its practice under which a debt doubled or tripled if a debtor defaulted, could result in the ruin of the borrower. And with the financial ruin and possible enslavement of poor borrowers the consequences would be communal friction. So the reason for the ban on riba was undoubtedly to preserve and maintain harmony, unity, and cohesiveness in the Muslim community of 7th. Century Arabia.

Context is crucial in interpreting the meaning of any discourse. It is especially important in interpreting the meaning of Quranic verses. It is widely believed that many of the verses of the Quran came in response to the needs of the Muslim community, living in a particular time and space, and/or to deal with a particular problem. It is our responsibility as rational beings—we are instructed by God to use our brains—to grasp the meaning and contemporary relevance of

Islamic verses concerning riba. Remember most people in the 7th century Arabia were quite poor, probably living near subsistence levels. Therefore all borrowing were motivated by need, individuals in distress needing to borrow from rich people, not to take advantage of an investment opportunity, like a private equity transaction, setting up of plant, or a leverage buyout. Such one sided relationship resulted in abuses—excessive interest and probably even doubling or tripling of the principal amount in the event of non payment on time—and it is in this context that we must interpret the prohibition against Riba. In light of this, in interpreting the word riba, it is important to keep in mind the historical circumstances in which the Quran was revealed to the Prophet (PBUH) in the Seventh century. The word riba almost certainly, applied only to lending to the poor and destitute. Put differently I would suggest that in order to understand the true meaning of a word in the Quran, we have to make an attempt to see what it meant in the 7th. Century Arabia, not what it means today, when the nature of investment and lending practices has changed dramatically from that time. Indeed rich people were advised to give free loans (as opposed to charging interest) for the sake of God. Furthermore it says in the Quran that if a debtor is in difficulty, then delay things until matters become easier for him and going on to say that if the lender were to write off the debt as an act of charity that would be better for the rich lender. The Quran, indeed, aimed at helping the poor and to introduce greater equality in society, in addition to prohibiting usury, it also imposed Zakat or wealth tax on the rich. Thus it seems clear that in the verses concerning riba, the Quran was addressing lending and financing of poorer members of society, when money was advanced for consumptional purposes; riba or exploitation of the needy thus through charging of excessive interest became a sin. The central message of Quran is one of compassion and justice. This being the case, a money lender charging excessive, and prohibit ably high interest rate—usury—would be acting against the principles of justice and compassion.

Against this background, and moving forward some 1400 years, I would like to relate the essential parts of a financing transaction from first hand experience. In the mid 1970s during the reign of the Shah of Iran, Iran Air wanted to purchase a number airplanes manufactured by Boeing. The Airline and the Central bank wished the planes to be financed with a loan of about $400 million by commercial banks in conjunction with the Expert Import Bank of the United States and asked the leading banks to submit their proposals. Given the excellent credit rating of Iran and the shortage of good lending opportunities in the Middle East, fourteen international banks sent in their proposals. The competition to win Iran Air's business was so intense that a number of banks even sent in their Chairmen to make a pitch to senior officials in the Iranian government, including Bank Markazi, the central bank. Even David Rockefeller, the Chairman and CEO of the Chase Manhattan Bank made a special trip to Iran to see his friend the Shah of Iran.

In my own meeting with the Vice Governor of the Central Bank, he told me that he had received a call from the Palace asking the Central Bank (it had the responsibility of arranging the financing on behalf of Iran Air) to give the mandate for the transaction to Chase if its offer was reasonably competitive. Fortunately for my bank, Chase's offer was not very attractive from the point of the Central Bank. Still, to make our offer even more attractive, at the suggestion of the Central Bank, I gave them a new letter, with improved terms and conditions and got the mandate to lead manage this financing.

The point of this story is that in this case there were fourteen banks jostling for Iran Air's business—indeed tripping over each other—prepared to lend to this airline with the finest terms and conditions. Consequently, because of its excellent credit rating, reputation and standing in the market place, the borrower was calling the shots. To put it more bluntly, the borrower had more leverage than the banks, clearly a situation vastly different than that existed in the 7th. Century Arabia. Again, remember the injunction against Riba came to ensure that the lenders would not exploit the poor borrowers by charging them exorbitant interest and/or fees.

In this situation is Iran Air a poor or weak borrower? Are the banks exploiting Iran Air by charging them an interest rate of ½ % over LIBOR (essentially 1 /2 % over the cost of money to the banks), barely enough to cover the expenses of the banks? So in this situation who is exploiting whom?

Returning to the question of riba, let us read some of the Quranic verses relating to riba to see their relevance to present day financing transactions and the negotiating positions of both lenders and borrowers:

Al Baqarah 2:276-280: God has allowed trade and forbidden usury. Whoever on receiving God's warning, stops taking usury may keep his past gains—God will be his judge—but whoever goes back to usury will be an inhabitant of he Fire, there to remain. God blights usury, but blesses charitable deeds with multiple increase: He does not love the ungrateful sinner. Those who believe, do good deeds, keep up the prayer, and pay the prescribed alms will have their reward with their Lord: no fear for them, nor will they grieve. You, who believe, beware of God: give up any outstanding dues from usury, if you are true believers. If you do not, then be warned of war from God and His Messenger. You shall have your capital if you repent, and without suffering loss or causing others to suffer loss. If the debtor is in difficulty, then delay things until matters become easier for him; still if you were to write it off as act of charity, that would be better for you, if only you knew".

Al-Nisa 4:161: "And for practicing usury, which was forbidden and for consuming the people's money illicitly. We have prepared for the disbelievers among them painful retribution";

Ar-Rum 30-39:

"The usury that is practiced to increase some people's wealth, does not rain anything at God. But if you give to charity, seeking God's pleasure, these the ones who receive their reward many fold".

From these verses three points are obvious: One, that a borrower is assumed to be the weaker party—a poor person. Two, in light of this assumption, God's orders to the rich money lender are that he should show compassion in giving the borrower more time to repay the loan if the debtor is having a difficulty in paying the loan when due and going so far to say that in a such a situation it would be better if the money lender forgave the loan altogether. Third, God is instructing Muslims to give to charity. In other words instead of lending money, rich Muslims are advised to be charitable toward the poor member of the society. This message is repeated several places in the Qumran.

Fortunately, the translation that I am using above refers to riba as usury—excessive or exorbitant interest. But for the sake of the argument, even if one were to take riba to mean normal interest, would the Iran Air type of transaction be covered by the verses of the Quran? As I have shown Iran Air was not a poor borrower. If any thing it dictated the terms to the bankers. Quite a switching of roles from the circumstances of the 7ᵗʰ century Arabia. Second because of the strong bargaining position of this particular borrower, it was able to extract extremely favorable terms and conditions from the banks. As a matter of fact many bankers participating in the syndicate told me that because of the extremely thin margin over the London Interbank Offered Rate, they did not expect to make a profit; they were only participating because at that time it was prestigious to lend to Iran. Again, in this circumstance what exactly was wrong in charging a normal and market rate to Iran Air?

Proponents of Islamic banking might say that this transacntin can be structured in an Islamic fashion by "Islamic lease financing". Even if the borrower was willing to lease the planes from the banks, the real question is would it make any difference to the borrower in terms of cost of financing? The answer is no because the Islamic banks in structuring a transaction along Islamic lines would use the same margin over their cost of fund and/or the interbank rate to structure the transaction. In light of this what is the point of structuring a transaction of this type using an Islamic mode of financing if the borrower is not going to benefit, in terms of intent rate (cost of money), term of loan, or the sharing of risk? Why create additional paper work, solicit opinion of Sharia boards, if the underlying substance of the transaction is going to be the same as in a conventional bank financing? Put more simply, is there additional value being created by structuring a transaction to make it Sharia compliant by giving it Islamic labels?

A criticism leveled against the conventional banking system is that by lending money at a fixed or a floating rate (over say, the London Interbank Offered Rate or the U.S. Prime Rate) the banks do not assume any risk; all risk, say the proponents of Islamic banking is assumed by the borrower. In other words, the banks do no share in the risk of the business. There is only one problem with this superficially compelling argument: it is wrong and spurious. As a former senior lending officer for a major international bank, and a senior member of the bank's credit and loan policy committee, let me explain why. The conventional banks want their clients to succeed in their businesses because when the customers fail, the banks don't collect on their loans. And that is the reason every bank will set aside a certain amount of reserves to cover losses from bad and doubtful loans. These run into billions of dollars every year. Such reserves and/ or write offs naturally result in the banks making less money for their shareholders. Therefore the banks want their clients to succeed because when the clients don't, the banks also lose money. In that sense banks do share the risk of businesses they finance with their clients.

I will give the reader a specific example to illustrate the point: In the late 1970s, when in response to the Iran-Iraq war the price of oil shot up from about $20 a barrel to about $35 a barrel, a number U.S oil exploration companies decided to borrow substantial sums to finance their exploration and drilling operations. The price of oil was going up so steadily that a consensus developed among economists that by the end of the 1980s the price of oil would reach $60 a barrel. On the basis of this assumption, the banks (including the bank where the author worked) in New York and other places lent billions of dollars to oil companies. But after the loans had been disbursed the price of oil began to drop and went as low as about $11 a barrel by mid 1980s. You can guess what happened next. The small to medium size oil companies declared bankruptcy because under their set of assumptions, and given their operational costs, they needed a minimum price of about $40 a barrel to make a profit and to generate enough cash flow to service the debt. So when the price of oil dropped dramatically, the banks wrote off billions of dollars in loans. To compound the problem oil companies were not the only borrowers wishing to take advantage of the expected increase in the price of oil. Real estate developers borrowed money to build office buildings to provide office space to the oil industry in Oklahoma and Texas and they also built homes to house the new workers. The reader, I am sure has already guessed as to what happened to loans to the real estate industry. Indeed those lead to the collapse of the savings and loan industry which resulted in the United States government spending about $500 billion to rescue this sector of the economy. Commercial banks losses were on top of this amount. The point of this example is that it was not the borrowers who suffered alone; the commercial banks shared in the pain. If anything, the commercial banks took the brunt.

The reader may well ask why the banks were so stupid. It is a good question. In reply I will say, that the bankers are not terribly bright people, they simply want to follow the other banks, a sort of herd mentality. If one bank's management in the above example had reached the judgment that the assumption regarding the future price movement was faulty and unrealistic, other banks would have been prepared to lend money. In all banks that I know of bonuses and pay increases are given to those lending officers who do deals, not to those who go against the conventional and majority held view.

Yet another example should prove to the reader and I hope to the proponents of Islamic banking that Western commercial banks do share in the risks of business with their borrowers. Again during the time the reader was a senior banker in New York, one of largest customers declared bankruptcy under chapter 11 of the U.S. bankruptcy Code. This particular customer, having noticed in the real estate boom of the late 1960s, that the state was actually importing cement from foreign countries, decided to borrow some $200 million from a syndicate of banks (including $50 from the bank where the author worked) to expand the capacity of their cement plant. By mid 70s, however, the economy had turned in the wrong direction with the net result that the demand for cement plummeted and the company was in trouble. It filed for Chapter 11 of the U.S. Bankruptcy Code, under which it asked the bankruptcy court to permit it to stop making interest and loan repayments for the time being until it could devise a plan of re-organization.

A colleague from my bank and I spent one full year on this "loan workout" and the other lenders and creditors had assigned similar teams. We could have forced the bankruptcy judge to permit the banks to foreclose on the assets but that would have resulted in the plant closing, workers losing their jobs, and owners' equity being completely wiped out. Instead our goal was to permit the company to continue to operate under the direction and supervision of the U.S. Bankruptcy Court. What is more, the banks lent additional money to support the continuing operations. The idea was to buy some time, for the economy to improve and also to sell some non-essential assets. In the end all parties working together were able to agree on a plan of re-organization, resulting in saving of jobs; the banks received most of their loans back, and the owners were permitted to preserve a portion of their capital. The point of this story is that the banks do share in some fashion the risk of the businesses they finance and that they are not always guaranteed to get the loans and interest paid in full. Finally when things do turn sour, most banks do work with their clients. The fact that God saw it fit to advise Muslim money lenders to give more time to borrowers if the borrowers were not able to pay on time, adding that it would be better for lenders to altogether forgive the loan, probably means that most, if not all money lenders were pretty ruthless in 7th. century Arabia.

That said, does usury—exorbitant and/or exploitative interest— exists in contemporary times? Absolutely. Most notably it is quite prevalent in the credit card industry in the United States. Many credit card companies, including some of the largest banks in the United States, charge as much as 20% p.a on outstanding balances to some of their customers—those that were not able to make all payments on time and or had exceeded their lines of credit. American credit card debt currently runs into hundreds of billions of dollars and a fairly high portion of this amount is at these rates, which can be regarded as usurious because the cost of funds to the banks is on average less than 4% p.a. That leaves an obscene mark up of 16%. Even taking into account for reserves for possible loans losses, it still leaves the banks with extremely healthy margins.

In the United States usury laws are state laws that specify the maximum legal interest at which loans can be made. As a matter of fact until a few years ago, many states had laws saying that lenders could not charge more than 12% p.a. on their loans. However, when in the inflationary environment of the 1980s when the Prime Rate was higher than that, some states, notably North Dakota, in order to attract credit card back office operations and to create employment opportunities for their residents, revoked their usury laws. With this flexibility some of the banks from New York moved their consumer lending and credit card business to these states, which permitted the banks to charge as much as the market would bear. Today of course in the very low interest rate environment the credit card companies have not seen fit to lower their interest rates. Because all credit card companies charge essentially the same rates the consumers— especially the poor ones-are left with very few choices. The affluent ones, either pay their bills in full and/ or because of their better credit they get better terms and conditions.

The United States Congress has opted not to regulate interest rates on purely private transactions, although it arguably has the power to do so under the interstate commerce clause of Article 1 of the Constitution. It is however, a federal offence to use violence or threats to collect usurious interest (or any other sort). Such activity is referred to as *loan sharking*, although that term is also applied to non-coercive usurious lending, or even to the practice of making consumer loans without a license in jurisdictions that require licenses.

With the exception of some of the credit card debt and pay day loan companies' loans, interest today is considered a fair bargain in most of the Western economies. And if you look at the home financing loan rates in the United States (6% for a 30 year fixed rate loan), home equity loans and student loans, they are downright bargains, enabling consumers to purchase their own homes and educate their children.

AN ANALYSIS OF MAIN ISLAMIC BANKING INSTRUMENTS AND PRODUCTS

Islamic banks in order to undertake the banking business in an Islamic way—Sharia compliant is the term they use—have come up with a number of Islamic banking products. A sharing of risks—a profit and loss sharing—with the borrower is supposed to be the underlying premise of these modes of financing.

There are essentially following four modes of financing:

1) Mudaraba
2) Musharaka
3) Murabaha
4) Ijara (lease financing)

Mudaraba:

Under Mudaraba an entrepreneur is entrusted with funds for investment by one or more investors. The concept is that the entrepreneur—a bank or a businessman—will combine the funds with his knowledge, hard work and time and engage in a business activity, such as trading or a project to produce goods etc. If the business is successful, the entrepreneur will return a pre-specified share of the profits plus the capital to the investor and keep the balance for himself for his efforts and time. In the event there are losses, they are all for account of the investor; the entrepreneur's loss is his time and effort. In practice very little—probably as low as 1-3%—of Islamic banking business is done using this mode of financing.

Musharaka:

Musharaka is very similar to Mudarba and the only difference is that under the Musharaka, the entrepreneur, addition to contributing time, effort, and expertise also contribuees some capital to the venture. And because the entrepreneur is risking some capital, presumably his share of the pre-specified profits will be higher than in the case of the Mudaraba.

Both of these modes of financing meet the test of Islamic banking: a sharing of risks and a partnership arrangement. Indeed these modes are very similar to the venture capital industry in the Western world, especially the United States. In the United States the venture capital industry has fostered the growth of many industries, including the high tech sector. In fact the development of such companies as Netscape, Hewitt-Packard, Sun Microsystems, Google, Apple, Cisco, is entirely due to the financing made available by the venture capitalists to entrepreneurs, engineers and scientists. This financing is made available by venture capitalists—as partners—because of potential profitability of proposed new ventures. A bank on the other hand, in making a lending decision is exclusively interested in the creditworthiness of the borrower. It should come as no surprise to the reader that if the founders of the above named companies, as well as hundreds of others in the advanced economies, had gone to the banks for loans to finance their projects, they would have been shown the door. Therefore it is safe to say that had it had not been for the venture capital industry, many innovations and companies in the high technology sector would have not existed. In the U.S. venture capitalists invest some $25 billion a year in new projects as partners with entrepreneurs.

By comparison, while stated principles of Islamic banking are similar to those of the venture capital industry and Mudaraba and Musharaka meet the requirements of Islamic banking, in practice, neither of these modes of financing has absorbed a significant share of Islamic banks assets. In fact based on writer's own observations and experience at one of the leading Islamic banks, as well as private conversations with other Islamic bankers, I would estimate that no more 5% of the Islamic banks assets are employed on these two modes; currently the Islamic banks control about $300 billion in assets.

Murabaha:

Perhaps keeping in mind that the Quran encourages trading to riba—interest or usury—, Islamic banking have come up with a mode of financing known as Murabaha, or a cost plus profit contract. Essentially it involves the bank, at the request of the client (borrower) purchasing specified goods from a third party and then turning around to sell the goods to the client (borrower) at the purchase price plus an agreed fixed profit margin. The idea is that the bank purchases the goods at one price, takes legal possession for some time, and then sells the good at a higher price to its client. The higher price includes a profit, which is pre-determined and fixed. In theory it sounds reasonable and appears to be consistent with the principles of Sharia. Certainly structure of these transactions meets the letter of the law. However, whether they meet the spirit of the Sharia is another matter.

As practiced by the Islamic banks—and again the writer has witnessed this at first hand—the central problem is that the banks keep their ownership periods very short. It may not amount to more than a few seconds for a vast majority of transactions are closed simultaneously much in a way of a back to back letter of credit is handled by the banks. What is more, since their ownership period can be measured in seconds, the banks do not assume any operational risks, normally associated with trading activities. Indeed in practice unlike a real trading transaction, the banks purchase the commodity or goods only after the customer has agreed in writing to purchase it from the bank at a profit. The bank does not assume any risk, including risk of the goods. The bank however gets a pre-determined fixed rate. This is clearly interest, concealed in Islamic garb and therefore not conforming to the requirements of the Shariah, certainly not the spirit of the Sharia.

There are additional problems with this mode of financing:

1) The Islamic banks in determining and calculating their "profits" on Murabaha transactions operate within the framework of conventional banking benchmarks such as LIBOR etc with the result that at the end of the day, the net result for the client (borrower) is the same as in a conventional banking borrowing:

the cost of funds to him is the same as if he had borrowed from a conventional commercial bank. If this is the case what is the point of the whole exercise? The modes of Islamic financing were designed to deal, at least in theory with the injustices alleged to be present in conventional commercial banking. As structured and practiced, has Murabaha made the transaction more equitable? The answer would have to be a flat no.

2) Murabaha historically was a crude trading practice designed for transactions between real sellers and real buyers involving physical goods, mostly commodities. Banks are not trading organizations; they take deposits from the public and either lend or invest such funds as custodians. By structuring a financing transaction and disguising it as a trading transaction the banks are simply trying to fool someone. Would God look to such trickery and deception on the part of the banks with compassion and kindness?

3) Islamic finance proponents claim that in the conventional banking transaction the customers are saddled with all the risk of the business, with the banks taking none of the risk. This of course is patently false, because the conventional banks see many of their loans go bad, or un-paid and that is why they set aside a percentage of net income to offset against doubtful or bad loans. That said Islamic finance is supposed to be handled on risk sharing basis with the banks' clients. Yet virtually all Islamic banking transactions using the instrument of Murabaha are fully secured and collateralized by goods, land, shares etc. As a matter of fact most Islamic banks only lend 80-90 % of the value of the assets. So what risk are the Islamic banks taking that the conventional banks do not take?

As an example, it was recently reported in the Middle East press that Etisalat International, the investment arm of Emirates Telecommunications Corporation, will raise $2.1 billion through the Islamic finance industry to finance the acquisition of a 26% stake in Pakistan Telecommunications Company. The 18 month bridge facility will be structured as a "share murabaha" using the underlying shares of PTCL for the trade transactions to affect the financing. Let us briefly analyze this transaction: One, it is structured as a "trade transaction". Is there really a trade here and or the transaction is being simply dressed in Islamic garb to make it appear Islamic? Two, the banks will hold shares as collateral against which they will be financing 90% of the market value of the shares. The share price PTCL will have to drop by more than 10% before the banks assume any risk. Third, the pre fixed profit or the mark up on this so called trade transaction is likely to be same as the interest cost of a conventional bridge loan, collateralized with shares of a public trading company. So from the point of view of the Etisalat International is there any difference in the cost of financing or the security it has to provide to the banks? None whatsoever. Given this why go to all the trouble creating additional convoluted documentation to make it appear Islamic? Is this the best Islamic bankers can come up in the way of innovation in Islamic finance? While in the West, venture capitalists are financing—as partners, with no collateral or security—entrepreneurs with new inventions in high technology, bio technology and other industries, Islamic bankers are busy giving new twists to murabaha mode of financing that serves no real purpose, finances no new industries, or create new jobs. It should be stressed here that about 80% of the $300 billion Islamic banking business is done using this mode of financing.

Ijara (Islamic Lease Financing)

Known in some countries as Ijara, this instrument is essentially the same as lease financing in western countries. Under this method of financing the bank purchases a piece of equipment (airplane, truck, machinery etc) and rents it to a client for a specified period of time at a mutually agreed upon rental rate. The rental rate reflects the cost of the equipment as well as the time value of money—interest. The Islamic scholars have blessed this Shariah compliant because at least in theory there is some risk sharing because of the ownership of the equipment by the bank. However, in practice the Islamic banks require the equipment to be insured (with the insurance premiums to be paid by the client) and banks, like their counterparts in the West also require that the client put up some of the money—in practice financing no more than about 90% of the cost of the equipment.

In order to establish their credibility and to demonstrate their
relevance and their creative abilities the Islamic banks are always busy
with new Sharia compliant products. The latest example is a $1 billion
oil and gas financing for Dolphin Energy, to be funded by 15 banks.
The four year financing facility, according to the lead banks is
structured as an *Istithana* transaction in which Dolphin (the borrower
or lessee) enters into an agreement to construct the portion of the
project relating to the transportation system on behalf of the Islamic
banks, and enters into a forward lease agreement for the use of these
assets. This transaction is being hailed by the lead banks as
innovative—a feat of financial engineering—sounding like the
Islamic banks deserve a Nobel Prize because the" transaction will set
valuable precedents that will serve as benchmarks for Islamically
structured project financings for years to come". In spite of this hyped
up talk, and despite its pious sounding name of Istihana, the
transaction is no different than if a conventional bank had agreed to
finance an Airbus plane, to be built by Airbus, purchased by, say by a
bank and leased to say, Emirates Airline. The fundamental problem
with this transaction and the reason it is not really Sharia compliant,
despite its being blessed by a Sharia Board is that it is lacking in the
essential element of sharing of business risk—ownership risk, if you
prefer, that would have come into picture, if the deal had been done
on a Musharaka or Mudaraba basis. The banks are still getting a pre-
determined rate of return and all the risk falls on the shoulders of
Dolphin Energy, especially when factored in the collateral and the
insurance. So through these various devices—mostly cosmetic—banks
end up with virtually no risk. If the Islamic banks, label their
hamburger, a Mecca burger, as long as it still has the same ingredients
as a McDonald's burger, is it really any different in substance? The
unfortunate reality is that while lawyers can craft documentation to
make a transaction appear Sharia compliant in letter, if the spirit is
missing, what exactly is the point of the entire enterprise? The bottom
line is that Islamic lease financing is the same as practiced by the
conventional banks with interest as an integral part of the financing
mechanism.

It is quite evident from a critical analysis of some of the more
prominent transactions, and based on my own first hand experience
as an advisor with an Islamic bank, that Islamic banks go to great

lengths to avoid risk, the very element they are supposed to share with their borrower/clients. Islamic banks have arrived at a wonderland in which through their creative use of language, there exists an Islamic equivalent to almost all the major products and modes of financing of the conventional interest based sector. Only the labels are different. They may have found loopholes to conform to the letter of the law, but the spirit of Sharia is sadly absent from their financial dealings and shenanigans. Even the granddaddy of all Islamic banks, the Islamic Development Bank, an organization set up as part of the Organization of Islamic States to promote economic development in the poorer Islamic countries, in its lending practices behaves just like the other privately owned Islamic banks. A good deal of its investment/loan portfolio, my friends in the bank tell me, consists of murabaha transactions, many to finance oil exports from Saudi Arabia to the less developed counties in the Islamic world. As a matter of fact, instead of increasing its profit and loss basis portfolio as a percentage of its total portfolio it has been going down in recent years, so much so that it is currently probably no more than one percent. So over 90% of IDB's portfolio is in lease financing and murabaha—both based on interest, although in the case of murabaha transactions clearly disguised as profit or mark up. Notwithstanding Islamic Development Bank's pious statements and pronouncements this is a deception and dishonesty at a massive scale.

ROLE OF ISLAMIC CLERICS IN ISLAMIC BANKING

The history of Islamic banking is not a long one. It is a relatively new construct, less than thirty years old, despite the fact that Quran's ban of riba now being widely quoted by dozens of Islamic scholars came down some 1400 years ago. The idea, as part of a larger Muslim identity concept, first originated in India in the late 1930's and took off in earnest in Pakistan when Zia ul Haq became the leader of the country in 1977. Indeed if any religious scholar can be considered the intellectual father of Islamic banking it would probably be Syed Abdula Mawdudi and on the political front Zia ul Haq of Pakistan was the first head of state to order in 1979 that all banks in the country must stop charging interest on their loans and conduct their lending/ investment operations on a profit and loss sharing basis.

The genesis of the idea came about when Muslims in India were debating whether they were Muslims first and Indians next or the other way around. A few Muslim scholars argued that to be a Muslim was to live differently from Hindus and Sikhs and that Islam offered a complete guidebook to all domains of life, including science, art, medicine, law, politics and economics. Mowdowdi in particular maintained that Islam offered a complete way of life, that within the Quran and Hadith there were answers to any problem or issue a Muslim faced in the world. All Muslims had to do was follow the Quran and the Hadith, set up proper institutions consistent with the teachings of the Quran and Muslims would be able to have just, fair, honest and efficient institutions that would also help to unite the Muslims.

Zia ul Haq in 1979, in order to stay in power and expand political base, decided to embark on an Islamization program in Pakistan. Being a dictator and thus lacking legitimacy, he felt that by supporting

Islamic ideas and causes, he would get the support of the religious scholars who in turn would be able to tell their audiences to support Zia because he was trying to be good Muslim ruler, following in the foot steps of the rulers who came immediately after the death of Prophet Muhammad (pbuh). Zia was not the first to exploit religion for dubious purposes. But he was so assiduous in harnessing the forces of religion to buttress his illegitimate rule, that he became the ultimate con act, false piety shoved down the throat of Pakistan people.

As part of this initiative in 1978 he announced that any laws passed by legislative bodies had to conform to Islamic law and any passed previously would be nullified if they were repugnant to Islamic law. In 1979 he established the Shariat courts to try cases under Islamic law. A year later, Islamic punishments were assigned to various violations, including drinking, theft, prostitution, adultery etc. Next came the process for the eventual Islamization of the financial system aimed at eliminating riba.

The job of implementation of Islamization of the financial sector fell to the Ministry of Finance, the Central bank and the religious scholars. Most of the them were blissfully unencumbered with any knowledge of banking, Islamic history and economics. As Ghulam Ishaq Khan, the Minister of Finance at the time himself told me they were ordered to convert the conventional banks (fortunately all state owned) to Islamic banks. They came up with a concept of profit and loss sharing (PLS) and mark up, interest disguised as profit. But the government sponsored program ended in total failure. What is worse is that if anything because of the additional paper work and documentation and sharia scholars opinions it has probably added to the cost of funds for the borrowers. The only people who benefited were Sharia scholars, members of the legal profession who were employed to draft new loan and investment contracts as well as printing presses which t got contracts to print new forms. In promoting his Islamic agenda, instead of breaking the shackles of the past, looking ahead, and building a modern and progressive state, Zia set the country back on a journey back to medieval times. And the country further declined in the area of scientific learning. The low point came when he sponsored a science conference aimed at studying ways to harness and produce electric power from gins. Later, as a consequence of this Islamization agenda, including the setting

up of madarasas—religious schools—and support of individuals who
would later form the Taliban, brought terrible misery, to Pakistan as
well to the world.

The "intellectual godfather" of Islamic banking, namely Moulana
Maududi has also been less than consistent in his views. For example
although he had stated that Islam offered a complete way of life and
that Muslims needed to maintain a separate identity he was against
the partition of India into two countries, essentially against the
formation of Pakistan. Yet, when Pakistan was established, he set out
to appropriate it, going on to insist that its laws, including economic
and financial had to conform to Sharia. Although Pakistan was created
to secure the rights of Muslims, it was not meant to be an Islamic
country in the sense that it was going to abandon the present laws in
favor of Islamic laws existing in the 7th century Arabia. The founder
of Pakistan in fact has stated very clearly that Pakistan was to be non-
theological in its laws and governance. But Zia and the Mullahs
hijacked the country and began a journey backward, insisting that
there was no difference between the Arabia of 7th century and the
21st. century. Since that time successive governments in Pakistan have
been unable and/or unwilling to stop the march toward gradual
fundamentalism and a literalist interpretation of the Quran. Here
then a question needs to be asked if Maududi did not see fit to have
a separate country for Muslims, how could he later advocate that
Muslims must have a separate economic and financial system—
Islamic banking—based on his interpretation of Islam?

It is ironic to note that the first Islamic banks on national scale
began in Pakistan—a non Arab country—. As a matter of fact Saudi
Arabia, the seat of Islam remained cool to the idea of Islamic banks
for many years. For example Faisal Islamic Bank originally wanted to
set up an Islamic bank in Saudi Arabia, and even though it had
prominent Saudi shareholders including Prince Mohammed Bin Faisal,
the Saudi Monetary Agency refused to give them the license to open
in Saudi Arabia. They opened in Bahrain. Nonetheless, following the
example of Pakistan other Muslim countries were under pressure to
allow the establishment of private Islamic banks and many did.

In promoting the establishment of Islamic banks, the Sharia
Scholars have played a critical role. Lacking any knowledge of
banking, economics and for many, even Islamic history, in

interpreting riba, they have confused interest with usury. If they had had any knowledge of Islamic history and capacity for critical thinking, and looking for meaning in context, they would have come to the conclusion that the Quran's injunctions concerning riba referred to usury, and not to normal interest. Secondly, as Sharia advisors to Islamic banks they have blessed many transactions as Islamic—meaning non-interest bearing—when in fact they are clearly charging interest, but interest payments are masked. I have first hand seen comical cases where the Sharia scholar of an Islamic bank only spoke and understood Arabic but a lending officer only spoke English and Urdu. A particular financing transaction was structured in English with such terms as x % over LIBOR. So we had an interpreter who would translate from English to Arabic, explaining this convoluted transaction to the Sharia adviser. It was at times painful and other times comical to watch this proposal being presented to this religious scholar for his blessing to ensure that it was consistent with the principles of Sharia. This "Sharia scholar", elderly and partly deaf, had little experience in modern banking and finance. However, mindful of the fact that the bank was paying him a generous retainer he gave his blessing to a deal, after being fully made aware that the bank wanted to do this deal, even though from the look on this face it was quite obvious that he could not tell the difference between a trade deal and a leverage buy out transaction. The fact that many of the so called Sharia advisers to the banks are nothing more than rubber stampers does not reflect well on the credibility and intention of the banks. It is clear that if Sharia advisers to Islamic banks are going to play a meaningful and constructive role, they must acquire sophisticated knowledge of banking and finance.

The thinking people around the world, especially in the Muslim countries have been too timid or politically correct not to speak out and say that what the proponents of Islamic economics are advocating is not workable or effective. We should be able to point out the failures and short comings of Islamic banking and economics without being accused of being anti Islamic. A modern economy is far more complex and sophisticated than the economy of the desert of Arabia that existed from 630 to the death of the fourth Caliph in 661—the period that proponents of Islamic banking and economics cite as their model and the golden age of Islam. Every mode of Islamic financing should be subjected to a process of critical analysis. There is an Arab saying that if God were to humiliate a human being it would deny him knowledge. And remember the Quran placed such value on education and knowledge that Muslims were instructed to acquire knowledge even if meant their having to travel to China (because it was considered the farthest place from Mecca and Medina). Instead Muslim clerics and proponents of Islamic economics choose to ignore the vast amount of knowledge in the West on how a modern economy works and the best route and policies for economic development and growth of employment.

But then I should not be surprised at the lack of critical thinking on the part of the Sharia advisers and scholars and Islamic economists. After all they have now gained power, prestige and employment. Dozens of Islamic clerics now serve on the Sharia boards of Islamic banks with very generous perks, travel allowance and retainers. Moreover a new industry of Islamic banking conferences and Forums has emerged, permitting hundreds of Sharia Scholars, bankers and economists to gather in all the financial centers of the world to hear each other speak praise each other for all the innovations they are making. As they say nice business if you can get it. But I hoping that someday someone will have the courage to tell the participants, especially the Islamic banks, to stay home and donate the money to poor people. This single act on the part of the Islamic banking community would do more to alleviate poverty in the Muslim world than all the empty and useless talk at these forums and conferences. There are at least 5 large conferences per year and these have been going on for at least 25 years, and each easily costs more than 2 million. That is more than $200 million, enough to educate and feed thousands of children in Africa.

Sharia advisers to Islamic banks, either out of ignorance, lack of education and an understanding of Islamic history and banking or to preserve a measure of power and influence have played a less than constructive role in two major areas: First in declaring that all interest is riba, they have confused interest with usury, thus inflicting a costly experiment on Muslims. In the process they have helped create and inefficient, costly, and cumbersome banking industry that is incapable of performing the functions of modern banking. Second, by blessing the murabaha mode of financing as Islamic they are permitting Islamic banks to engage in deceptive and dishonest practices.

The problem is that many Sharia scholars have assumed the role of self styled experts on matters and issues related to Sharia, especially Islamic banking. The subject has become their exclusive domain. And they interpret Islam's progressive and forward looking religion in a very narrow, rigid, and static framework. The reality is that it is too important an issue to be left exclusively in their hands. The Central banks must become more active in regulating the activities of Islamic banks and the regulatory authorities must also take steps to insure that just as managements are subject to approval of central banks, Shariah advisers to Islamic banks must also receive approval of the banking authorities to ensure they are qualified. Conventional bankers, historians, economists and other thinking people must also begin to play a more active role in the debate surrounding Islamic banking issues.

In light of the conflicting fatwas and rulings coming out of different Shariah boards on the same subject or type of transaction, Central banking authorities must help to set up a National Sharia Board in each country. These boards must consist of well educated Sharia scholars—both in banking and religion—and they should be paid by the Central bank to insure their objectivity. Individual Islamic banks may still keep their own Shariah boards but in all respects their rulings, decisions, fatwas etc must be consistent with the rulings coming out of the National Shairah Board.

ISLAMIC BANKING AND ECONOMIC DEVELOPMENT

Google was started in 1997 by two graduate students in computer science at Stamford University. They came up with a simpler and faster way to conduct searches on the internet. To finance their venture they raised $100,000 from an angel investor and later were able to secure $25 million in venture capital financing from two venture capital firms in the Silicon Valley in exchange for a 10% stake in the company.

Today, some seven years later, about 60% of the searches on the internet first take place on Google. The company employs 4000 people and has a market capitalization of about $79 billion. That is seventy nine BILLION dollars. The fact that it employs 4,000 people is the most significant part because these employees, being well paid—and many also shareholders of the company—are able to buy homes, feed their families, educate their children, and purchase consumer goods. And through the process of a multiplier effect, the recipients of their spending—grocery stores, car dealerships, home builders etc—in turn are able to benefit and they in turn contribute to the creation of more wealth and jobs. The fact that it has created a very useful technology which benefits users in numerous ways and that it created over $70 billion of new wealth—with the two founders becoming billionaires and venture capital firms making a fantastic return on their $25 million investment—are simply a nice bonus.

This story is only one of many. Since the start of Industrial revolution in England and later in the United States, these economies have created millions of new jobs and given birth to new technologies and new companies. Since the 1980s alone in the United States such companies, to name just a few, have emerged simply with an idea: Hewitt Packard, Sun Microsystems, AOL, Yahoo, Intuit, Netscape,

Google, Apple, Microsoft, EBay, and Amazon. These companies were largely financed by the venture capital industry and now employ, directly and indirectly millions of people. Indeed during the Clinton presidency alone, about 20 million new jobs were created. Equally significant the venture capital industry by teaming up with bright engineers, scientists and entrepreneurs created in the words of John Doer, "the largest legal creation of wealth in the history of the planet". As a result of encouragement of research and development, innovations in technology, and availability of abundance of venture capital, the United States has been able to create new jobs and keep the unemployment rate to manageable level of about 5%.

By contrast, human development indicators in the Islamic world are among the lowest in the world; poverty is pervasive, literacy is less than 50%; unemployment is high; and institutions of higher learning are insignificant. Even in Saudi Arabia, the largest oil producer in the world, I am told by my friends in the banking industry and government; over 30% of the country's college graduates are unemployed. The situation in the non-oil producing countries is much worse. What is even more puzzling is that Islamic world which until the 13th century was at the forefront of scientific and technological innovation, has not generated any new ideas, innovations, inventions, experiments and movements necessary for sustained economic development in the last 700 years. When one travels in the Islamic world these days all one sees are familiar logs and trade marks of the West: Coke, Pepsi, Microsoft, IBM, McDonalds, Pizza Hut, Mercedes, Dell, Nokia and others. Where are the Islamic world's inventions and products?

Against this backdrop, two questions need to be asked: Islamic banks, by staying away from interest and by sharing risk with their clients, were supposed to help make the economic system more just, fair, equitable, and honest. Second, implicitly they were supposed to promote economic development of the Islamic world. Have the banks achieved any of these goals and objectives?

Sadly the answer is a resounding no. There is absolutely no evidence that the Islamic banks have made any contribution in either of these areas. As far as the economic development issue is concerned, because virtually 95% of the Islamic banks' loans carry interest— disguised in ingenious ruses—the outcome and consequences as far as the economy is concerned is the same if they had charged interest openly or if the same borrowers had borrowed from conventional banks. The outcome and consequences might have been different if a significant portion of their loan portfolio had been invested in a true profit and loss basis and/or they had financed entrepreneurs with ideas, innovations and new inventions etc. But lending to relatively large and state owned entities, like, the Emirates Airline or the State Trading Corp of Pakistan, the Rice Corporation of Pakistan (with the guarantee of the Central Bank of Pakistan) on a murabaha basis is not going to help in promoting economic development or requires great credit analysis skills. Western banks and local conventional banks would have been happy to lend to these companies on an openly disclosed interest basis. Can the Islamic banks point to any value they have added by lending to these companies on a murabaha basis? Sure by engaging in "trading" they may have complied with the letter of the law (trading is preferable to riba) but what about complying with the underlying spirit of the law?

The responsibility of governments in the Islamic world and the Islamic banks should be to promote dynamic development, prosperity, poverty reduction, employment generation, expansion of production, science and technology education, health and human resource development. Have the Islamic banks played any role in promoting any of these goals in the last 30 years?

With respect to the second point of helping to make the economic system more just, fair and honest, Islamic banks' contribution is equally dismissal. Indeed, if anything by themselves engaging in deceptive, hypocritical lending practices and fostering trickery they can be accused of promoting dishonesty. Many verses of the Quran instruct Muslims to be truthful, so Islamic banks by promoting dishonesty and duplicity would appear to be committing a grave sin against Islam. I suppose the really valid question is: in the eyes of God which is a greater sin, charging a reasonable interest openly, even if one equated riba with interest, or engaging in deceptive, hypocritical and dishonest lending practices?

Islamic banks often cite that the main reason they do not "lend" (invest) on a truly profit and loss basis (venture capital) is that because the business community in the Islamic world has low business morals, that the businessmen can not be trusted, and more specifically they tend to keep more than one set of books. Second reason cited by my former colleagues is that the bankers lack the expertise and time to monitor the affairs of businesses involved in industries which requires technical and specialized knowledge.

While the first reason may have some merit, I would say that on the basis of my experience most of the younger, especially Western educated people in the Islamic world tend to follow the business morals of the West, believing and practicing in norms of transparency, honesty and trustworthiness. Second reason is simply fallacious; Islamic banks can hire the right people if they wanted to and can also find the time to monitor their operations, if they wanted to.

The real reason the banks are not engaging in investing on a venture capital basis—profit and loss sharing—rests with their laziness and unwillingness to assume risk. It is far easier, safer, and prestigious and even lucrative in the way of bonuses, if an Islamic banker can get a mandate to lead manage a financing along Islamic lines for, say the Emirates Airlines, as opposed to investing in couple of young entrepreneurs with ideas whose ideas may not result in profits for the banks for several years. So the over riding motive is short term profits, publicity, safety, and prestige. Naturally Islamic banks can not be expected to make any constructive and meaningful contribution to economic development, add additional value, or even practice true and genuine Islamic banking until they get away from this mindset.

That said there are of course always exceptions and two come to mind. These are Arcapita Bank (formerly the First Islamic Bank of Bahrain) and Gulf Finance House. Both are less than 7 years old. Both operate similar to private equity firms in the west. And in their "investment "operations they act as partners, sharing in the risks and rewards with their clients and/or co investors. What differentiates these two institutions from their Islamic banking colleagues is their professionalism and staff. Unlike other Islamic banks, which are by and large staffed by commercial banking types, these two, especially Arcapita, are largely run by highly sophisticated, bright and experience investment and merchant banking professionals, with an entrepreneurial bent. So to a large extent what sets apart Arcapita, from its competitors are its corporate culture and the quality of management talent assembled by the bank. At the end of the day a bank is all about people—its staff—, not the size of its balance sheet or its ability to offer so called Sharia compliant products. These two have shown to the marketplace that it is possible to do most of their business on a true profit and loss—partnership-basis and still show very attractive returns for their depositors as well as their shareholders. The vast majority of Islamic banks engaged in conventional banking type of lending in disguised form, would do well to follow the example of these two banks.

Since the start of the industrial revolution, financial institutions have played a leading role in promoting and financing economic development. Financial institutions, acting as intermediaries, between savers and borrowers make the capital available to finance new inventions, factories and businesses, thereby creating jobs, and promoting economic development. At an international level, poor governments borrow from rich countries as well as multinational institutions like the World Bank to finance large scale industrial projects, to create jobs, and to alleviate poverty.

This being the case, if the Islamic banks have chosen to replace the conventional banking system with an Islamic banking system, they must address satisfactorily the following two issues:

One: Are their banking practices contributing to economic development? Put more plainly, if the loans made by Islamic banks—with Islamic labels—had been made by conventional banks, would that had made any difference to the borrowers in respect to cost, benefits, and terms and conditions? In other words, are their banking practices adding value? If not, then the contribution of Islamic banks would appear to be zero.

Second, are the banking practices of Islamic banks helping to promote justice, equity, compassion and fairness among the Muslim communities? After all that must have been the rationale for the prohibition against riba in the Quran. Again if the answer is no, then exactly what is the purpose of building this industry, this house of cards? Isn't it the time to say that if all the Islamic bankers can do is talk the talk but can not walk the walk, they should consider shutting down their operations; it is time to shout that the emperor has no clothes.

VENTURE CAPITAL

The stated principles of Islamic banks—favoring profit and loss sharing over interest—are very similar to the financing techniques used by the venture capital industry in the West. Islamic banks are supposed to act like venture capital funds, financing as partners, and individuals with good ideas, who do not have collateral or powerful connections to get loans from conventional commercial banks. But in practice, Islamic banks invest only a tiny portion—less than 2%—of their portfolio in mudaraba and musharaka transactions which are based on the concept of profit and loss sharing; the balance of 98% of assets of Islamic banks consist of murabaha and Ijara (leasing) modes of finance, which in the view of many carry interest concealed in Islamic garb. In other words Islamic banks go to great lengths to shun risk—something they are supposed to share with their clients.

By contrast, although the United States is not an "Islamic" country by conventional definition, in spirit and in real terms, its financing institutions offer more Sharia compliant financing and investment than that provided by all the Islamic banks combined. American venture capital firms provide in excess of $25 billion per year in equity financing to help finance development and growth of thousands of new startups in health care, technology, information technology, and other promising industries.

Indeed there is no better example of Sharia compliant financing than venture capital finance. Venture capital allows entrepreneurs to build a firm without having to borrow and pay high interest charges before they generate any revenues. It is a process of cooperation between entrepreneurs and venture capitalists, with risk sharing an essential element. Entrepreneurs provide the bright ideas, and hard work, while venture capitalists furnish the money—either their own or that of their clients—as partners, not lenders. Simply put, if the business succeeds both benefit and in case it fails the entrepreneur is not obligated to repay the investment. This is the essence and spirit of Islamic finance.

Conventional banks are different from venture capital firms in three respects: First while the bank bases its lending decision on the credit worthiness—balance sheet, collateral etc—the venture capital firms focus on the potential viability and profitability of the proposed venture. Second, the conventional bank earns interest on its loans, whereas the venture capital receives share of the profits. In the West typically the real return to venture capital firms comes when the new venture does an IPO at an attractive price. Third, unlike the banks, the venture capital firms actively advise and assist the entrepreneur in executing the project by making introduction to other firms, and bringing in consultants etc. A recent example of the later contribution is that of Google. In 1999, in addition to giving the two young founders—both PhD candidates at Stamford University—$25 million in venture funding the venture capital firms of Kleiner Perkins and Sequoia Capital, convinced that Google needed to hire an A list CEO, encouraged the founders to hire Eric Schmidt, a well respected technology executive. Before joining Google he had been the CEO of Novell, and before that for nearly fifteen years he was a senior executive at Sun Microsystems. Later, the venture capital firms also brought in Bill Campbell, a former CEO and Chairman of Intuit as well an Apple board member and regarded as one of the most respected executives in Silicon Valley, as a senior advisor to the company. His nickname was the Coach—a reference to both to his past as a college-football field general and his sideline as an informal management adviser.

The point of telling this tale of Google is that this company started in 1998 by two precocious grad school nerds at Stamford University with $100,000 provided by an angel investor and later funded to the tune of $25 million in venture capital funding, today employs 4,000 people and has a market capitalization of $80 Billion—twice that of General Motors. The transformation of the company, a process started by introduction of new technology—a simpler way to search the internet—was coordinated and managed by the two venture capital funds who in addition to providing the money—for a 10% stake in the company—more crucially brought in senior advisers to guide the development of the company.

Venture capital system has played a leading role in the industrial development of the United States. How is industrial innovation financed in the U.S.? The answer is that a smart engineer or a scientist undertakes path breaking research—occasionally financed by the Federal government—at a major university, starts a company with the expert assistance and financing provided by a venture capital firm and later they jointly take the company public at a huge price, benefiting both parties. Scores of Silicon Valley companies including modern day giants such as HP, Intel, Sun Micro Systems, Apple Computer, Netscape, Intuit, Compaq Computer and Cisco Systems were financed by the venture capital industry in the form of equity capital. All were created in the last twenty five years from ideas grounded in science and technology. Scientists, engineers and entrepreneurs came up with the ideas, research and inventions, while the venture capital industry provided the funds on a partnership basis. Significantly as a result of this cooperation millions of new jobs—20 million during Clinton's eight year presidency alone—have been created in the United States.

Venture capital gives the U.S. a creative and forward looking dynamism that few nations can match because it is rooted in the very foundation of the country. In this regard America's most important advantage is a willingness to take risks. By contrast if a scientist or an engineer with a new idea or invention wanted to raise financing to develop his idea or invention into a business in the Islamic world it would be virtually impossible for him to find funds. He would be told by a conventional bank or an Islamic bank to first produce some collateral.

It was not always so. From 750 CE to 1100 CE, the golden age of Islam, science and technology in the Islamic world far surpassed that of Europe. The Europeans learned from Muslims, especially through contacts with Muslim Spain. Muslims made original inventions. This was made possible by a culture and environment that encouraged learning, research and invention. The enlightened rulers and probably also wealthy families helped by funding research and sponsorship. Today most technology used in the Muslim world comes from outside the region. It seems that native springs of invention have dried up and nothing of mention has been invented in any of the Islamic countries in the last two hundred years! Muslims that once led the world in science are dropping behind at a rapid rate in scientific research and information technology.

Many factors were responsible for the fall of the Muslim civilization beginning around the 12th century, but a single act on the part of the Ottoman Empire deserves special mention. It relates to the printing press invented by Gutenberg in Germany in 1455. This invention brought about a major revolution to communication and to the tools of learning. The Ottoman rulers instead of taking advantage of this new technology forbid printing and this restriction remained in force until 1727. By contrast, in earlier times, when the books had to be hand written, the city of Cordoba in Spain— where the Muslims ruled for several hundred years until 1492— had dozens of free libraries carrying thousands of books. So the decline began when the Muslims stopped learning in clear violation of the Quranic teaching to acquire knowledge even if one had to travel to China.

The problem is not with intelligence and creative abilities of Muslim youth because thousands of Muslim scientists and engineers have managed to excel in the West. Many own large computer and other technology companies. Others have made significant scientific discoveries in medicine and various technologies for government, universities and corporate labs. Venture capital industry largely financed those who decided to go into business, in developing and bringing their products to the market. This then is the crucial difference between America and Muslim countries. If an American team of engineers or scientists has an idea about a new product or application, they can easily get venture capital investment. In Muslim countries very little, if any, risk capital is available.

I would, therefore, advance the thesis that a major factor in the Islamic world's underdevelopment is the non availability of suitable financing for entrepreneurs. If the leaders in the Islamic world are truly interested in improving the living standards of their people, gaining economic independence, regaining their pride and days of glory, they must encourage original discovery, research and invention and devise ways to finance young entrepreneurs—possibly along the line of venture capital financing. This encouragement, among other things, must come in the form of setting up of several venture capital firms in the Islamic world because that would send a message to scientists and engineers that promising companies can obtain financing from venture capital firms on a partnership basis.

Islamic banks are in a unique position to make a beginning in this direction. In fact the stated principles of Islamic banking are the same as those of venture capitalism. Islamic banks, like the venture capital firms, are expected to participate in the risks of the businesses they finance. But in practice much of what passes for Islamic banking these days may not be consistent with the spirit of Sharia. Islamic banking is currently a $300 billion industry. The question is: Have the Islamic banks since their inception in the 1980's made any contribution to the development of the economies of the region, lifting the standards and creating new employment. There is no evidence that it has made the least bit of difference and/or created additional value. If the same deposits that reside with the Islamic banks had stayed with the conventional banks because of the similarity of lending practices of Islamic banks and conventional banks, the performance of the economies would have also been the same. That is because Islamic banks like the conventional banks also shun risk and largely lend on Murabaha basis to state owned and larger well established companies on a fully secured basis, who are able to obtain financing on similar terms from conventional banks.

The Islamic banks need to truly differentiate themselves from conventional banks. And the only avenue open is the route of venture capital. It has two advantages: one, venture capital is consistent with the stated principles of Islamic banking, and second, that promotion of venture capital financing would result in original research, development in science and technology, creation of new businesses and employment. Islamic banks may want to set up separate venture capital funds—the need is for at least $10 billion—within their organizations and use these funds to finance on a truly profit and loss sharing basis individuals—scientists, engineers, entrepreneurs—with bright ideas, and help to transform the Middle East economies into exciting high growth, high tech and full employment economies.

In closing it is worth noting here the advice, Eugene Kleiner, the father of venture capitalism, offered both to entrepreneurs with idea and to venture capitalists: To idea men looking for money he said:" First get the facts straight. Second don't lie. Third, leave nothing out.

Fourth, seize cash as soon as it is offered" And since he knew the other side as well, his advice to venture capitalists was that "they should look less at ideas, than at the soundness and energy of the people peddling them. Great ideas could easily fall apart on paper or worse still in the marketplace. Make sure that the dog wants to eat the dog food". John Doer, another noted venture capitalist (his venture capital company, Kleiner Perkins, has financed many of the well known technology companies offered this advice to novice venture capitalists:" If you like the founders and you like the technology, price does not matter". So the core point of venture capital is that while ideas are important it is the people that really matter: Venture capital firms invest in people.

IJTIHAD AND ENLIGHTENMENT

One of the crucial topics for discussion in the theory of Islamic Law including Islamic economics and banking is the right to ijtihad. Ijtihad means "reasoning or interpretation". It is generally believed that the right to use an independent judgment on the source of dogma was cut off in the Sunni sect of Islam in the tenth century, or possibly couple of hundreds later. This is often referred by the term "the closing of the door of ijtihad". In these centuries freedom of innovation, exploration and critical thinking ended as the rulers, in order to maintain a tighter control over their subjects, declared that independent judgment was no longer permissible, that all answers were available, and that one needed merely to follow and obey. What made it worse was that as a result of these edicts people became afraid of expressing new ideas and argue new approaches to problems and issues of the day to day life.

Before the door to ijtihad was closed, Muslim economies were booming and more economically and technologically advanced than the West. Indeed during between 700 ads to about 1500 it was Europe that was living in the dark, and after learning from the Muslim they began their assent. The West's rise started with the Toledo school of translators when the scholars started translating Arabic books into Western languages. Universities were established at Bologna, Oxford, Paris, and Cambridge. Soon Europe in 13th century was in the midst of an intellectual awakening, and culminating in the beginning of Renaissance in the early part of the 14th Century. This led to an age of exploration and discovery in the 15th century, followed by Reformation in the 16th. Century. After that there was no stopping the West as it began its long and sustainable journey to scientific and industrial revolution in the 17th century to present.

The point is that the European progress began with interaction with Muslim societies through Spain. Later when the Europeans were making advances in science and technology, Muslims failed to learn from the Europeans, and led by the Ottomans opted out of the exploration of the intellectual world. The lesson for the Islamic world is that interaction between societies and cultures is the most powerful engine of change. The Muslims must learn from the West, as they had learned from the Muslims.

If Muslims wish to enter the modern world and wish to become part of the world community, it is imperative that Muslim scholars reopen the door to ijtihad. Such reopening would enable scholars to reinterpret the Quranic verses, especially relating to riba, keeping in mind the historical circumstances—the state and nature of the economy and lending practices—in which the Quran was revealed to the Prophet in the seventh century Mecca and Medina. The core point is that Muslims must be able to use their critical thinking faculties and reasoning in order to understand and reinterpret the Quran and apply its message to suit the new conditions of modern age. For example, in interpreting the riba injunction in the Quran one must keep in mind that there were no banks at that time, that most borrowers borrowed out of necessity, not to take advantage of an investment opportunity, that there were no manufacturing plants, and that the only type of business activity involved trading. Such trading activities consisted of stand alone single transactions wherein a trader would purchase goods in say, Mecca, and sell them in Damascus and on the return journey the trader would purchase different commodities in Damascus for sale in Mecca. And that is the reason the Quranic verses show a preference for trading because that was the only business activity available at that time; there were no factories, banks, joint stock companies. The list of what was not there in the 7th century Arabia is endless. The Muslim world must live in the real world—today's world—not the fantasyland of the 7th. Century Arabia.

It is widely understood that most of the verses of the Quran came in response to and as guidance to emerging situations or conditions faced by the population or the Prophet (pbhp). And as it relates to Riba please remember that virtually all borrowers needed to borrow out of distress and need. By contrast today's borrowers come in all shades and sizes. Take the Leverage Buyout Industry (LBO). The principals of LBO firms do not need to borrow to pay rent, buy groceries or even to pay for their children's school tuition. They borrow because by combing their equity capital and with borrowing at rates of say 7-10% pa, they can acquire companies, restructure and improve their operations and then sell them at a profit, generating an average annual return of in excess of 30%. And this is after they have paid the banks for the cost of the loans. First such investment opportunities did not exist during the time of the prophet. Second, it is virtually impossible to structure such transitions on a purely PLS basis, and even if the banks were prepared to do it the LBO firms may not be interested. The central point is that as in this example and the earlier one concerning Iran Air, how relevant or reasonable is the ban on interest, if riba is taken to mean interest?

As I am writing this, I came across in the papers another private equity (LBO) transaction. This one relates the proposed sale of Hertz, the nation's largest car rental company by Ford Motor Company to a consortium of private investors for about $15 billion in cash and debt. At a purchase price of $15 billion, it is probably the second largest private equity/LBO transaction, the largest being the sale of RJR Nabisco in 1989 for $25 billion. The private buyers of Hertz, following a typical transaction pattern, will probably not put up more than 10 to 20% of their own capital; the rest will be borrowed from the banks. One observation and then a question: Unlike the disadvantaged and poor borrowers of 7th century of Arabia, no one is forcing this set of private investors to borrow this staggering amount of money to finance the purchase of Hertz. Second how would the proponents of Islamic banking handle this financing without charging interest? Or should they as matter of generosity give away the depositors funds which they hold as custodians and intermediaries? The private equity borrowers are a sophisticated lot and clearly they plan to make a great deal of money on their investment by improving and restructuring the operations of Hertz. In view of this would the banks be exploiting this borrower if they charged them normal interest to finance this transaction?

Another major difference between the economy of 7th century Arabia and today's world needs to be kept in mind and analyzed. And that is the money lender of 7th. Century Arabia lent his own money whereas today's lender is simply an intermediary, acting as a custodian for the deposit holders. Presumably depositors have saved their money—let us say for their retirement—and they wish to receive a return on their money by letting another person or institution use the funds in a profitable venture. Let us further suppose that the only alternative available to them is "trading", because that is a permissible activity. How realistic is that for an elderly couple? What is wrong with the idea of your collecting a fee—call it interest—from a person or institution to whom you permit them the use of your capital (and we are not necessarily talking of a poor and destitute person from the 7th. Century Arabia)? I would suggest that in interpreting the Quranic verses one must use the "ethical or justice criteria". We know God is just. That means He is just to both the borrower as well as well to the lender. Is the lender, an individual or a bank acting as a custodian for a number of people, expected to lend to people without charging a fee or interest? How just would be that arrangement to the savers? Again, not every transaction can be done on a "trading" basis.

Elsewhere in this book, from my personal banking experience I have related couple of financing transactions to show their modern complexity and to raise questions whether the Quranic verses relating to riba could be expected to shed light on ways to structure such modern financing transactions. Apart from those types of private transactions, if the verses relating to riba are interpreted to mean simple interest, how would one handle loans from the World Bank to third world countries to promote economic development and alleviate poverty? How would the IMF be able to lend, say $10 billion to Turkey, to balance of payments stabilization purposes without charging at least a minimum rate of interest? Did the Quranic scriptures revealed in the 7th century anticipate such financing needs on the part of sovereign nations? And a more specific question to the religious scholars and Islamic bankers: how would you handle a loan from the IMF to a sovereign country like Turkey on a "trading", or "profit and loss sharing" basis? The simple and straight answer is it can't be done.

The Western economic scholars and economists beginning with Adam Smith have made a tremendous contribution to an understanding of economies, economic development, consumer behavior, role of interest and monetary policy etc. These advances have enabled the West to innovate, industrialize, create jobs for its citizens and improve the living standards of its citizens.

Two examples are worth noting here: Firs the Roosevelt Administration in the 1940s in order to get out of a prolonged recession decided to take a proactive role and decided to put people to work on public works jobs, including new roads etc. The government following the advice of the noted economist Keynes, financed this activity by issuing bonds. This was a first in history where a government was borrowing—thus adding to public debt and deficit—to put people to work so that they could earn a dignified living. The policy was successful. It resulted in the country getting out of a recession. If the government had not played an active role, it would have gone on far longer, resulting in more misery, starvation and death of children from malnutrition. Here a creative use of borrowing—entailing paying of interest—made an eminent sense.

Second, after the Second World War, the U.S. government came up with a policy statement that all families should be able to own their own home. To implement this policy it devised a scheme to enable families to borrow up to 30 years from banks, agreeing to purchase these loans from banks, if they wished to sell such to the government, creating bond markets to trade in these instruments and finally allowing all interest payments on their home loans to deduct these from the U.S. tax bills. So the government essentially subsidizes the purchase and financing of private homes. The home buyers ended up with lower interest cost, very affordable for majority of home buyers. As a result of this creative policy, new trading and borrowing instruments, tax policy and a cooperative arrangement between the government and the banks, over 80 percent of Americans currently own their own homes. This is in sharp contrast with other countries where most people live in rental homes, partly because, in most counties a family wishing to purchase a house must have savings almost equal to 100% of the purchase price of a home. Government financing, with very low down payments, along the lines available in the U.S. is virtually non existent in most other countries. To repeat, in the U.S. home financing is made possible through the creative use of interest. In this situation which has made possible for millions of Americans to own their own homes is charging interest exploiting the poor, unreasonable, unjust or unfair?

Islamic countries must learn from the West's economists and bankers. Islamic jurisprudents using the concept of ijtihad—reason and critical thinking—must come up with more rational and pragmatic interpretations of riba, in light of today's complex financial dealings and systems and needs. What would make sense is perhaps for the relious scholars to agree that in each Islamic country, an interest rate that is no more than say 2% over the cost of funds for the banks, or X percent over the Central Bank discount rate, or x percent over the LIBOR is permissible. Anything over that would be regarded as riba, meaning usury. Empirical evidence shows how poorly most notions of Islamic banking and finance have fared. The experiment of Islamic banking has failed. It is in a sense a spent argument. In light of this, the proponents of Islamic banks should reform the system before they are subjected to more ridicule.

To give the reader a sense and level of cynicism that prevails in the international banking world, one only need to observe the furious pace at which some of the most prominent Western banks have jumped onto the bandwagon of setting up Islamic banking subsidiaries. As much as some Muslims may want to believe, it is not because these Western banks subscribe to the view that Islam offers a "complete way of life" and that by extension Islamic banking is superior and more moral way to conduct business; it is simply because they see an opportunity to make money. They are in it because these institutions sense an opportunity to attract deposits at cheap rates and lend and/or invest the deposits at very attractive rates. And they and their regulators, including the Federal Reserve Bank and the Comptroller of the Currency, also know that in the final analysis Islamic banking is no different than conventional banking, meaning their Islamic banking offices will be charging interest and assume no greater risk than if they made straight loans, even if cosmetically the loans are described as murabaha or PLS transactions.

What should come as even a greater shock to Muslim Islamic bankers is that the Western owned Islamic banks are often able to attract deposits at cheaper rates and with less marketing effort that their purely locally owned Islamic Banks. Second, western owned banks like Citibank and HSBC are able to get mandates to lead manage the larger and more sophisticated transactions, thus earning the lion's share of the fees as well as getting good public relations converge. And from the client's view—both depositors and borrowers—they can have their cake and eat it too, because in their scheme of things they are dealing with an Islamic bank and the fact that it is a large Western international bank, provides them with security and access to sophisticated services. So if the object of the proponents of Islamic banking was to escape from the Western owned banks, they have clearly failed in doing so. It is not due to the cleverness of the Western banks; it is because in setting up a sham and deceptive Islamic banking system they left the door open for conventional banks to come and do business, as long as they changed the nomenclature. If on the other hand Islamic bankers were truly doing Islamic banking—sharing risks and partnering with their clients on truly profit and loss sharing basis—Western owned banks would have not touched Islamic banks would have avoided entering this market, because they too would have found it risky, and their central banks and bank examiners would have frowned upon that business. So the fact that dozens of Western banks have set up Islamic banking windows or subsidiaries to engage in Islamic banking has only one message for Sharia scholars and proponents of Islamic banking: we beat you at your own game—and in your own backyard.

Having made the foregoing observations and raised some questions, a final question still needs to be asked. Why is their a rush to set up additional Islamic banks? What exactly is the motivation on the part of locally owned Islamic banks? Is the Islamic banking system truly superior to the conventional banking system in the sense that it is more equitable, fair, and compassionate and is better able to help improve the living standards of the Muslim community? Why do the proponents of Islamic banking and Sharia scholars expect the four short verses of the Quran relating to riba (concerning themselves primarily with lending to the poor, charity, and compassion) to shed light on complex financing situations that would develop 1400 hundreds later? What are the reasons Islamic scholars and proponents refuse to acknowledge that the Prophet and the Muslim community of the 7th century Arabia lived in a particular time and space, with specific needs and circumstances? Those circumstances and needs of the community required a certain message and guidance. In light of this does it not make it sense for the scholars to interpret the verses relating to riba keeping in mind the context, the special circumstances of the time? What is the reason for their refusal to live in the contemporary real world? Why this desire for a backward journey to the 7th. Century Arabia? What is the motivation for taking one word—riba—out of the Quran, and give it a twisted interpretation and embark on this pious sounding expedition called, Islamic banking, which has not befitted anyone and/or added value.

I take it back, at least partly. The movement toward Islamic banking has benefited two segments: One, some governments and government leaders (as noted earlier Zia ul Haq, the former military dictator of Pakistan was a notable beneficiary) by using these moves toward Islamization have been able to increase their power, appeal and stay. And in this venture they co-opted some of the religious scholars who were happy to share in the new found power, prestige, not to mention monetary incentives, for after all many of them currently serve on the boards of Islamic banks as Sharia advisers.

Second, the owners, sponsors and managers of Islamic banks have clearly benefited from the phenomenon of Islamic banking. By using pious sounding labels for their products, the banks are able to attract deposits at relatively low rates from gullible and innocent Muslims and turn around and lend at attractive interest rates to borrowers, making a nice profit for themselves. Bonuses and good salary packages follow. Shareholders of Islamic banks are happy too. Since much of Islamic banking is done on a secured basis at very attractive interest rates, they benefit from receiving generous profits and dividends. For all intents and purposes Islamic bankers and religious scholars promoting Islamization, and Islamic banking are on a gravy train. In that sense the world of Islamic banking operates like a 'secret society" with its own lingo, codes, lofty rhetoric and pious sounding designed-to-obfuscate products.

Will there be any reformation, a move towards more rational and contemporary interpretation of the Quranic verses relating to riba in the near future? One hopes that if enough thinking people show the will and courage to voice their misgivings, calling for serious scholarship of the subject, it's quite possible. I certainly am hopeful that it will happen—the Islamic banking movement will reform and turn itself into a major innovative force.

The really sad and tragic conclusion that emerges from the performance of Islamic banking system is that apart from the two narrow classes mentioned above, it has not benefited the depositors, the borrowers, or the Muslim community, in terms of adding value.

Borrowers pay the same interest rate, as they would to commercial banks, under various religious guises. Depositors do not receive any higher return compared to what they would receive on their deposits with commercial banks. And finally the community as large has not benefited, because the poorer members are not able to borrow from the Islamic banks for lack of collateral; Islamic banks make very few, if any loans on Musharaka (venture capital-joint venture) basis; and their lending practices have not made any difference to improving the level of honesty, fairness, compassion and equity in the Muslim community.

Before the Muslim community in their zeal to set up even more and more Islamic banks and before the process goes so far in the wrong direction that it would be difficult to turn back to the real world—the world of the 21st century, there is a need for intellectual environment hospitable to the open and honest exchange of ideas. And as part of this process Islamic banking practices and proposals should be examined and analyzed like any other economic system and activity. To exempt the Islamic banks from a close analysis and scrutiny would not be doing the Islamic banking movement a service.

It should be clear to the reader that by expressing some misgivings about Islamic banks I am not calling the Quran into question (certainly I have no desire to invite a fatwa against me accusing me of being ignorant, anti Islamic, or misguided); I am simply arguing that the Quranic verses dealing with riba can be reinterpreted as in the past many scholars have interpreted riba to mean usury or exploitative interest, whereas proponents of Islamic banking insist that the only valid, true, and authentic interpretation is theirs, meaning that Quran prohibits all forms of interest. The Islamic economists regard the issue settled for all time. That should not be acceptable to any thinking person. Will there be any reformation, enlightenment, a move towards more rational, less rigid and literal interpretation? One hopes that now that we have a 30 year history for Islamic banking for examination and analysis, if enough thinking people show the will and courage to voice their misgivings and insist that the issue be subjected to serious scholarship it is quite possible that Islamic banking movement will reform and turn itself into a major innovative force for good. The Islamic banks could finance openly some businesses that could not be done without the element of interest but by and large—as proposed elsewhere in this book—become genuine venture capital firms, financing innovation, new discoveries, inventions, and entrepreneurs and start a new Islamic renaissance.

Indeed at this stage we need to make one point clear. It is becoming increasingly clear that many clerics and proponents of Islamic banking believe that the "golden age" of Islam was the period during which the four caliphs—also known as the 'rightly guided'—ruled after the death of Prophet Muhammad (pbuh). They regard this period as ideal—the best human beings can achieve. Implicit in this thinking is that there was equality, justice, fairness and compassion during this period. This is pure fantasyland; the reality is different. Although Islam in general made great strides in spreading the message, it was also a period of dissent and wars. In fact in the short period of some 30 years, three of the four caliphs met their deaths at the hands of murderers—fellow Muslims. More importantly a 30 year period, in the long span of history, during which no enduring institutions were established or any advances made in the realm of science or even any improvement in the living standards of the Muslims can be called a "golden age".

The "Golden Age" of Islam came of course later. It came during the Abbasid Caliphate (750 AD.), Muslim Spain, Safavid Iran, Mughal India and the Ottoman Empire. These times, most notably the Abbasid period, were marked by, among other things, intellectual achievement. Islamic rulers did not wall themselves in self imposed intellectual or communal ghettos. As a consequence, scholars made important and original contributions to mathematics, astronomy, medicine, chemistry and literature. A number of thinkers and scientists played a very useful role of transmitting Islamic, Greek, and other pre Islamic books and fruits of knowledge to Westerners. Among other achievements in this sphere, the translators contributed to making Aristotle known in Christian Europe. These advances in science, technology and literature would ultimately provide the impetus for the European Renaissance.

As a policy issue, what was so special about these "Golden Periods" of Islam? What can we learn from them? It would seem to me that the factors that stand out include respect for education (including critical thinking and rational analysis), scholarship, original discovery, inclusiveness and tolerance. By contrast in setting up Islamic banks, the proponents of Islamic banking have opted for a "segregated and ghetto like" system that has made no meaningful contribution to the human condition. Their desire to model their banking practices on the basis of literal interpretations and the economy of 7th century Arabia, while riding in Mercedes cars and using Nokia cell phones is hypocritical at best. For the sake of consistency, if my friends in the Islamic banking industry truly want to replicate the conditions of 7th century Arabia—their Golden Age—I suggest they start commuting to work on camels! But seriously, their banking practices have done damage to society because by using deceptive designed-to-obfuscate-products and modes of financing Islamic banks are contributing to more dishonesty on the part of their clients. My principal problem with their practices remains that they have not added any value.

Policy Recommendations for Islamic Banks

An honest analysis of lending practices of Islamic banks would confirm that over 95% of the modes of financing employed by the banks entail interest and that their practices only differ cosmetically from those of conventional banks. When conventional banks, acting in a transparent manner charge interest, Islamic banks charge an equal percentage point or an amount and call it a "commission, fee, profit or mark up". This is outright deception. The second point is that this exercise does nothing to promote economic development, justice, fairness or honesty. Finally while the stated goals and objectives of Islamic banks are very similar to those of venture capital firms in the West, very little, if any venture capital investment is undertaken by Islamic banks.

In light of the above observations I would suggest that the banks undertake the following steps and measures to reform themselves.

One: Sharia scholars should interpret the prohibition on riba keeping in mind the lending practices existing before the Prophet Muhammad's time, the state and type of economy and the nature of loans at that time. In the judgment of this layman writer the riba mentioned in the Quran refers to usury, not normal interest. Indeed usury—excessive or exorbitant interest is unjust, and unfair. What is a fair interest rate? Most banks currently charge their best customers about 0.75 basis points over LIBOR. Perhaps each central bank could state that a maximum of two percent over some index (discount rate, Fed rate, or Prime rate) would be allowed; anything in excess of that would be regarded as usury or riba.

Two: Be honest and transparent in their dealings with their depositors and borrowers. Many businessmen in the Islamic world have to bribe government officials in order to conduct their business and many out of guilt feelings that they are participating in such un-Islamic practices then attempt to seek some form of redemption by placing their deposits or borrow from Islamic banks. The tragedy is that the Islamic banks are no better than the corrupt government officials for they too, by using many ruses, circumvent the prohibition of interest, thereby making the customers an accessory to a sin. A double whammy, although while dealing with the corrupt government officials they know they are engaging in a dishonest business practice; they are innocent when they deal with Islamic banks. They believe the propaganda and pious statement the Islamic banks put out about their business practices, mission, goals and objectives and their emphasis on business ethics. Simply follow the simple rule: call things what they are.

Third: Islamic banks should concede that there are many types of business loans that are not practical to do on profit and loss sharing basis. These include a loan for working capital purposes for on going operations of a company that has been existence for a very long time and is engaged in a wide variety of businesses. For example if IBM wanted to arrange a line of credit for working capital purposes, it would be virtually impossible to work out a profit and loss sharing arrangement acceptable to both parties. How do you value the new financing and its contribution to a company that has spent billons of dollars on research and development? How do you segregate the contribution, profits, expenses where so many functions are centralized? In such situations it is best to concede that certain loans would have to be done on conventional interest basis.

Fourth: Become actively involved in Venture Capital financing. There are two principal reasons why Islamic banks must increase their activities in venture capital area: One, even if they could agree that normal interest is not prohibited by the Quran, it would still make sense for the banks to increase their investments along venture capital lines, because it is the best way to foster the development of new enterprises, creation of new jobs. Islamic banks can make a significant contribution to Islamic world's economic development. Second under the prevalent view that all interest is prohibited by the Quran, venture capital financing is the only truly Islamic way of financing and investing, because the banks become partners with their clients and share in the profits and looses of the businesses they finance.

Whatever the reason for entering this business, it has benefits for all participants. Entrepreneurs find capital for their ventures because the banks are not insisting on demonstrated creditworthiness. Rather the banks look to long term profit potential. Islamic banks should benefit because they will share in the profits of the ventures they finance. Generally speaking many venture capital funds (read Islamic banks) make average annual rate of about 30% on their capital—much higher than the Islamic banks currently make on their Murabaha and Ijara modes of financing, where their return is usually no more than 2% over their cost of funds. On a return on equity basis, the banks make no more than 20% annually; investing on venture capital basis could boost these returns to close of 30% per year.

A venture capital market requires the simultaneous availability of three factors, the provision of any one of these is contingent on the availability of the other two. These factors are entrepreneurs, investors with taste for risk and specialized financial intermediaries. At least two are a must; the third will come to the party.

In the United States, wealthy individuals and institutional investors (like pension funds, university endowment funds) with a taste for risk provide the capital to the venture capital funds who in turn invest in promising ventures and new technologies. The Islamic banks can actually perform both of these functions: providing the risk capital (since their depositors assume the ultimate risk, they would have to make their depositors aware of it and sell this product to only those who have an appetite for this type of risk) and acting as financial intermediaries. Once venture capital financing including seed capital is available from the Islamic banks, the third ingredient— entrepreneurs—will emerge very quickly. Entrepreneurs in the Islamic world—as well as Muslim entrepreneurs, engineers, and scientists living in the West—will begin knocking at the doors of Islamic banks as soon word gets out that Islamic banks are looking for entrepreneurs to underwrite.

As a first step Islamic banks jointly should set up two funds: one an Incubator Fund and second a Venture Capital Fund. The Incubator Fund can be set up with $1 billion and the Venture Capital Fund (Musharaka Fund) would have capital commitments of at least $10 billon to really make an impact in the marketplace. Incubator Fund is the first stage fund while the Venture capital fund would come in once the concept and technology of a proposed venture has been tested and shows promise.

Emerging businesses face considerable challenges when bringing a new product or service to market. History shows that start-up have a significantly higher success rate when they have an established partner to provide financial and other support. The Incubator Fund—acting as a partner—would assist technology oriented and other entrepreneurial starts ups during their concept definition and development stages. This incubator fund would allow entrepreneurs to concentrate their limited resources on the development of their product/service by drawing upon the proven expertise and support of the incubator.

The incubator would be staffed with professionals in science, technology, computer science, and management professionals. This talent is available from Muslims currently working for the likes of IBM, Microsoft, other technology firms as well as large consulting firms like Booz Allen, Mckinsy, Accenture, Baring Point. With proper and generous compensation packages such individuals can be attracted to the incubator.

This incubator management team will then be able to provide expert business advice to their clients. This advice would include concept evaluation, business plan development, capital acquisition, strategic business and financial planning, and access to technology and technical support.

Additionally the incubator could also offer a variety of facility—related features to tenant companies, including: sophisticated laboratory space, offices and furnishings, use of business equipment, including copiers, fax machines, and computers, manufacturing and assembly areas, access to specialized equipment, conference facilities, resource libraries, and advanced telecommunications capabilities. In summary the idea is that an incubator will offer technology companies a comprehensive infrastructure to support their ventures.

Such incubator could become an important source of actual venture capital financing. Of course the main source for venture capital deals would come to the Islamic banking venture capital fund from normal sources. As mentioned above, once it becomes known to entrepreneurs, scientists and engineers that a venture capital fund is prepared to finance them on a true venture capital basis, there will be no shortage of business.

Fifth: Set up charitable foundations or a Fund with annual and periodic contributions from profits from the Islamic banks, and from private contributions. This would be consistent with the teachings of the Quran because in many places the Quran advises Muslims to be charitable. Indeed in the two verses relating to riba, the Quran advises Muslims to give to charity and that if a borrower is unable to pay when a loan is due, the lender should forgive the loan as a charitable act. Additionally rich people are ordered to pay Zakat, or wealth tax.

In time this Charitable Foundation and Fund could potentially have $100 billion. The income from the Charitable Fund could be used to give scholarships to deserving students, fund the setting up of research facilities at local universities in science, fund the establishment of incubator funds, loans at preferential rates and without requiring collateral to poor people who wish to set up small businesses, along the lines of the micro-finance bank set up by Mr. Younus in Bangladesh. Given the increase in the price of oil and resultant wealth in the Arab world, this would appear to be the best time to set up a such a foundation and /or a fund and besides it is the best way to help the poor and talented people, promote economic development, create employment, and advance education, science and technology and promote entrepreneurial minded people.

Here again, one can learn from the experience of the United States. The U.S. gets maligned around the world on a daily basis for its culture of capitalistic consumerism, fast food, loose morals and movies portraying violence and exporting this culture to the rest of the world. While some of this may be true, it is a pity that what is truly unique and good about America receives very little attention around the world. This is the tradition of philanthropy or to use simpler term, charitable giving, and how it has helped individuals and groups to improve the human condition.

In 2004—the last year for which such numbers are available—Americans gave $250 BILLION (equal to 2% of personal income or GDP) to charity. Individual contributions average about $175 billion, while the balance comes from corporate foundations and corporations. As regards recipients about 50% of the total was given to religious organizations (churches, synagogues, mosques etc) who use it to support various charities, welfare programs and for educational purposes. Educational institutions receive about $50 billion per year. Some of the larger gifts to educational institutions included a gift of $300 million form Martha Ingram to Vanderbilt University, a gift of $200 million form Alfred Mann to University of California at Los Angles and University of Southern California, a gift of $130 million from James Rogers to University of Arizona, a gift of $100 million from Sandy Weill (of Citigroup fame) to the Cornell University School of Medicine., to name only a few. Additionally prominent businessmen like Bill Gates have set up their foundations to help education and health around the world. He donated in excess of $25 billion to set up the Gates Foundation, making it the largest foundation in the country. And some wealthy families in fact, believing that too much money is bad for building character of children have donated virtually all of the family fortune to improve the human condition. One notable example of this are the founders of Hewitt Packard, who set up a foundation for medical research with $8 billion—leaving less than $100 million for their children.

American universities in particular, and other educational institutions in general have always taken a pro-active approach to fund raising; they simply don't sit around and wait for people to contribute. Since 1641, when Harvard College sponsored the first systematic effort to raise funds for higher education when it sent a trio of preachers to England on a begging mission to raise funds, American colleges and universities have organized fund raising campaigns to boost their endowments, raise funds for student scholarships, and generally to bridge the gap between income generated from tuition fees (tuition fees normally cover only about 75% of the cost of education) and the cost of running a college or a university. What is now surprising is the number of announced campaigns with goals of $100 million or more. Harvard in 1994 became the first university to raise $2 billion in a single fund raising campaign (Harvard's endowment now stands close to a staggering amount of $25 billion, thanks to fund raising campaigns and very attractive returns on the endowment, averaging over 20% p.a). This kind of money clearly gives an edge to American universities and colleges to conduct research, attract talented faculty by offering them very competitive compensation packages, offer student scholarships to bright students from underprivileged backgrounds and generally to embark on innovative programs.

Charitable institutions of many kinds, including schools, hospitals, orphanages and monasteries have of course existed for many centuries and in most parts of the world—sometimes as creations of princely authority but most often as religious institutions. Ancient Egypt, China, India and Rome had them.

Throughout history Judaism has honored the principle of individual charitable duty, and Jewish communities around the world today are notably philanthropic. Christian communities, Protestant and Catholic, have developed along with their churches a vast apparatus of schools, hospitals, orphanages, and other charitable institutions that have flourished for many years. Muslims, as well, have a long philanthropic tradition. Today for example some twenty five thousand private endowments, known as *waqfs*, exist in Tehran alone.

In the United States a special aspect of this great tradition of charitable initiative has been the development of the private sector philanthropic foundation. Linked neither to government not to a religious body these foundations have taken initiatives and performed tasks far beyond responding to manifest needs and directly alleviating human distress. They thus represent a special form of social entrepreneurship and a potential for creative responsiveness to opportunities for human service. Such private sector philanthropic foundations exist in a number of countries around the world, but they are still preponderantly an American phenomenon.

About a century ago, as a result of the formation of the first great private fortunes in this country, and perhaps because of the heroic spirit of that age, a new kind of philanthropic foundation was created that has become a distinctive American achievement. The leaders were John D. Rockefeller and Andrew Carnegie. They poured a large part of their wealth into these new institutions. Adding inspired leadership, they demonstrated the immense potential foundations have for improving the human condition. The Rockefellers helped first to invent American philanthropy, then to institutionalize it, then to develop it to a fine art. Their generosity boggles the mind. Translating their $1.07 billion in donations into current dollars, the founding father John D. Rockefeller and his son John D. Rockefeller Jr. pumped the equivalent of $17 billion into doing good. To date only Bill Gates donation of about $22 billion to set up the Gates Foundation surpasses the Rockefeller generosity.

Among the institutions Rockefeller's millions launched:

> The Rockefeller Institute of Medical Research (which eventually became Rockefeller University) to find cures for contagious diseases;

> The General Education Board, to improve schools for blacks throughout the south;

> The Rockefeller Foundation, to tackle a host of significant problems, mainly in the areas of public health and medicine around the world; and

> The University of Chicago, a new standard setting center of excellence in higher education.

Rockefeller's philanthropy had its roots in his religious upbringing. He was a devout Baptist and saw himself as a servant of God. In his own words: "I believe the power to make money is a gift from God . . . . Having been endowed with the gift I possess, I believe it is my duty to make money and still make more money and to use it for the good of my fellow man according to the dictates of my conscience". Carnegie, the immigrant son of impoverished Scottish radicals, was impelled by gratitude to his adopted country (United States) and deep sense of social duty to help the poor and less fortunate to improve themselves and their condition. The decade from 1901 to 1911 was an explosion of one man's philanthropy the likes of which the world had never before seen. During this time he—the richest man in the world at that time—gave away $500 million which in current dollars would be equivalent of over $10 billion! His donations included funds for the University of Scotland to strengthen their research and teaching and to provide student scholarships, financing of thousands of libraries in the United States and abroad, the setting up of the Carnegie Institute to carry out a vast program of basic scientific research and the formation of the Carnegie Endowment for International Peace.

Today thousand of philanthropic foundations exist in the United States engaged in all kinds of programs. The Macarthur Foundation of Chicago undertakes one of the more interesting and intriguing programs. In addition to making annual grants of about $150 million for supporting innovative programs in such diverse fields as the environment, health, population and security issues, this $5 billion in assets foundation (set up by the Macarthur family who made their fortune in the insurance business) annually offers about 30 or so called *genius* awards to outstanding scholars, artists, human rights, scientists, environment activists, and journalists. The awards range from $250,000 to $500,000 depending of age. The Foundation views the awards as a gift, for whatever the fellow thinks will advance his life. They come with no restrictions and nothing whatsoever is expected of the recipient, although presumably the Foundation believes the award would free the recipient from the chore of making a living, thus freeing him to engage in more creative work. Since the program began in 1981, about 1000 fellows have received a total in excess of $250 million. A note to the reader: No one can apply for these awards; the Foundation through its "advisers" throughout the United States gets recommendations and the identity of the advisers is secret.

While earlier philanthropists made their money in industrial, insurance or banking enterprisers, technology is now the main font from which philanthropy flows. It is the source of wealth for many of top philanthropists of day. Some of the biggest donors of recent years including people like Gates (Microsoft), Paul G. Allen (Microsoft), Lawrence J. Ellison (Oracle), Jim Clark (Netscape), Pierrre Omidyar (EBay) David Filo (Yahoo) and John p. Morgridge (Cisco Systems) all made their fortunes in technology. So as mentioned elsewhere in this book investment in technology and promotion of venture capital can pay dividends in more than one way: First it enables entrepreneurs to engage in innovation and bring their products and ideas to the market, as the individuals named above did, in the process creating jobs and thus raising the standards of living of all participants. Second once they have made their billions of dollars, they help the community by donating money to improve the human condition.

No discussion on current American philanthropy would be complete without mentioning the role of Jewish philanthropy. The three million strong Jewish community, having a strong tradition of individual giving and being extremely active in philanthropy, probably donates from $6 billion to $10 billion a year for all kinds of charitable causes. One of the principal causes and beneficiary is Israel. Perhaps more than any other nation created in this century, Israel was built, molded and sustained by funds raised abroad, mainly from the United States. In fact about half of the money mentioned above subsidizes an array of agencies and help Jews in Israel. The remaining amount is donated in the United States for education, cultural and social institutions, museums, and hospitals. The community instead of relying exclusively on the government has a fine and noble tradition of looking after its less privileged members.

While current figures on American philanthropy are impressive enough, the future is even more promising. To give the reader some idea of what the future holds, as mentioned earlier Bill Gates of Microsoft fame and his wife, Melinda, have set up their foundation with a contribution of about $25 billion. The Foundation is focusing on programs in education and health. And he has stated publicly that most of his estate (currently worth about $75 billion) will go to charity. Warrant Buffet, another wealthy man, with a net worth of about $50 billion has expressed similar feelings. He goes even further in saying that he does not want to leave his children more than a couple of million dollars (presumably for purchase of a house) because he wants them to work as hard as he did in making his fortune. Again as mentioned earlier, a few years ago, David Packard (co-founder of Hewitt Packard) with a single stroke of the pen donated over $8 billion to set up the Packard Foundation to finance medical research.

Indeed many experts, on the basis of the rate at which new wealth is being created in the United States, predict that about $25 trillion in intergenerational wealth will be transferred over the next twenty years. Assuming people exhibit the same charitable dispositions as they have in the past, about $100 billon a year from estates alone over the next twenty years will go to charity compared to about $15 billion today. Once this sleeping giant begins to awaken, total giving could easily exceed $350 billion a year from the $200 billion per year for recent years. Clearly the best in American philanthropy is yet to come. So next time you hear someone maligning the people of the United States (criticizing the government of the U.S. is a different matter), remind them of the tradition of charitable giving in America and how it is making a difference in the lives of millions of people by improving the human condition.

I tell the story of the American philanthropy in some detail for couple of reasons: First, if the private sector and individuals had not been generous contributions and had instead relied exclusively on the government, the United States would never have become a superpower and leader in science, technology and education. Much of that was financed by private sector initiatives. This is most certainly true in the higher education sector. And it is American universities and colleges that have given the edge to the country over its competitors. The research and development that goes on in the top universities is far superior than compared to say Oxford and Cambridge, simply because top American colleges, as we saw above have huge endowments. Oxford and Cambridge, by and large rely on the U.K. government to fund its programs. And we know what happens when you rely on a government for your funding. As a result Oxford and Cambridge which at one time were the leaders in higher education have been left behind.

Second, while there are exceptions, wealthy Muslim families, especially in the Arab counties are not very generous in making charitable contributions to finance scholarships, education, research and development and generally to use their wealth to improve the human condition. To be sure most Muslims, in accordance with the teachings of Islam give 2.25% in Zakat, wealth tax, annually. That is not enough, certainly for families with billions of dollars in wealth. They should do more. And here the Islamic banks can lead the way by setting up philanthropic foundations because it is consistent with the teachings of Islam, is noble work and could lead to the improvement of the human condition in the Muslim world.

The focus of philanthropic foundations ought to be the promotion of scientific education. Education is the key. And since the governments in the Islamic world have failed to discharge their responsibilities it is incumbent on the private sector to begin to take the lead. While there are now some leading Muslims scientists—sadly living in the West—the Muslim contribution to scholarship and innovation remains extremely small in relation to the Muslim share of the world population. Prof Pervez Hoodbhoy, the leading Pakistani intellectual and expert on education, has noted that on a per capita basis that Arab scientific output is a mere 1% of Israeli scientific output. Although there are no exact figures available for the entire Muslim world, the same percentage would probably apply to the whole of the Islamic world. After all where are the Harvards and Yales of the Middle East, and how many PhD's in science the Muslim world is producing each year. Not many, I assure the reader. And when was the last time a new innovation in science and technology was made in the Muslim world? Not in centuries.

Muslims have learned to enjoy and appreciate McDonalds hamburgers, Pizza Hut pizzas, Pepsi, Coke, Western movies, to name some just some of the more familiar consumer products. Why can't they learn from the West the respect for education, the secrets and ways to set up first rate universities, set up foundations to finance research and development and give scholarships to needy and bright students?? I challenge that if the Islamic banks really want to do something truly Islamic and Sharia compliant this is the area they need to tackle. It is worth mentioning here that when some Muslim philanthropists have shown their generosity, they have started with misplaced priorities. One notable example of this is about a donation—if I recall correctly in excess of $100 million—a well known Saudi businessman made several years to set up a Business School at a prestigious and old university in the West. The university named the school after him, but that was most likely part of the deal. There are two things wrong with this donation: First, the West at this stage is not lacking in centers of higher learning, whether it is in business studies or chemistry; it is the Muslim world that is in dire need of first rate universities undertaking research and innovation. Second, it is in science and technology education that the Muslim world has the greatest weakness, not in business studies, marketing, and finance. etc. In other worlds if the gentleman had used his $100 million to set up a scientific research facility with endowment set aside for scholarships at a university in the Muslim world that would have been for more beneficial in the long term.

CONCLUDING THOUGHTS

Currently the dominant view among Islamic scholars, as well as some Islamic bankers is that Quran bans all interest. If one were to look at the Quranic verses in the context of the times, one would have to come to the conclusion that what the Quran prohibits is usury—exploitative or exorbitant interest. The Islamic scholars have made a mistake in equating usury with interest and by giving this ruling they are causing harm to all Muslims. The more disturbing point is that the current consensus view leaves no room for alternative interpretations concerning riba, whereas in earlier times Muslims debated this issue aggressively because of the respect for the intellectual satisfaction of puzzling through a complicated issue. Islamic scholars, especially those that are not on the payroll of Islamic banks (because by and large Sharia advisers to Islamic banks have become docile house pets), need to revisit this issue. For Muslims to continue to swallow almost uncritically the rulings from ignorant mullahs is wrong.

Islamic scholars have gone unchallenged by non-Muslim scholars because of the phenomenon known as "cultural relativism" and thinkers with different views have grown more timid for fear of offending the Islamic scholars and for fear that the mullahs would call label them un-Islamic, ignorant, misguided and pro-western if they questioned the dominant interpretation, however irrational or dangerous the consensus. In fact, as a result of this faulty ruling, the phenomenon of Islamic banking that has emerged is simply using slogans in pursuit of profits and greed; Islamic banks' lending practices are hypocritical, an insult to Islam and to human intelligence. The fact is that when one analyses most modes of financing of Islamic banks, the conclusion is clear: In their murabaha transactions (the dominant mode of financing), the difference between the purchase price and the selling price recognizes the time-value of money in the same way that charging interest does. Put more bluntly, Islamic banks charge interest on 95% of their financing transactions, but concealed in Islamic garb.

By charging interest using various disguises, essentially designed-to-obfuscate products, Islamic banks engage in deception, duplicity and thus promote dishonesty. The real question is: in the eyes of Allah which is a greater sin, charging interest openly or engaging in dishonest practices. Remember, in Islam honesty is a prized virtue and God in several verses orders Muslims to be honest. A bill of goods—interest—is being sold to both the depositors and borrowers in Islamic garb. An honest evaluation of Islamic banking, as currently practiced would seem to indicate that Islamic banks are terrible failures. Their lending practices differ only cosmetically from those of conventional commercial banks. What is more, while the stated principles of Islamic banking are very similar to those of venture capital form of financing, Islamic banks don't practice what they preach, with virtually no financing being done on venture capital and/or profit and loss sharing basis. Although Islamic banks have introduced a number of Sharia compliant products, with very pious sounding labels, if the truth be told they do not meet the standard of being Islamic in the sense that they are simply designed to conform to the letter of the law, not the spirit. The Islamic banks will no doubt dismiss the skepticism of this author but I would suggest that the real judge of their efforts is going to be history. The question they need to ask themselves with respect to any fancy transaction is whether the transaction will make the system more just, fair, and compassionate and in the end will it add any value and/or make any difference to the lives of the community?

That said, proponents of Islamic banking need to make a choice: either they should come up with a more moderate, less rigid and literal, and contemporary interpretation of the Quranic verses concerning riba, or they must make the Islamic banks conduct their business—without semantic gimmicks and tricks—truly on the basis of profit and loss sharing basis (essentially venture capital, mudaraba, and musharaka) and thus demonstrate and prove to the world that Islamic banking is a workable banking system. They can't have it both ways.

Printed in Great Britain
by Amazon